The Key That Unlocks Revelation

COPYRIGHT © Dr. Jimmy Henry   August 2020

Printed in the United States of America
All Scripture Verses are from the King James Version

All rights reserved by the author. No part of this publication may be reproduced, stored in a retrieval system, or transmitted in any form without the written permission of the author, except for brief quotations in critical reviews or articles.

Dr. Jimmy Henry
jimmyahenry@gmail.com

Dr. Jimmy Henry

Table of Contents

INTRODUCTION

THE KEY THAT UNLOCKS REVELATION
Revelation 1:1; 22:6

For centuries men have struggled to understand the message contained in the book named "The Revelation of Jesus Christ." Multiple theories have been advanced as to what the book says and means. Some become so disheartened with its many figures and symbols until they just close it and say it is too difficult to comprehend and they will just wait and see how it all turns out. Others have concluded that they know what it means and conjure up all kinds of spectacular events that they say are yet to take place on the earth.

Some try to use the news events of each day to interpret the messages contained in the book. We hear all kinds of elaborate stories about how, very soon, the sky will break open and the literal body of Jesus will descend in the clouds and every eye in all the circular world will see Him. Following His descent, the world will radically change and a new heaven and earth will be created upon which men will live for one thousand years, at the close of which it will all be destroyed and eternal heaven will begin.

Some prophetic writers have become millionaires writing about the things they say that are to take place when Jesus comes again. Their books sell like hot cakes because people have a natural curiosity about what the future holds. Most of them have set dates and tell their readers that time is short and very soon, from their day, Jesus is coming again. When their date comes and goes and nothing happens, they do not apologize, they just regroup and set another date and say get ready, "Jesus is coming soon." For the first forty of my ministry I preached that message.

But is that what the book says? Or are these views just the results of man's imagination running wild and predicting things that are not actually set forth in the book? Is the Revelation a description of what is yet future or is it a record of that which took place in Israel two thousand years ago? Are we yet to see the rise of a man called the Anti-Christ who will rule the world for three and one half to seven years, or is the one called the beast in Revelation 13 a historical figure who was contemporary with John? Could John have been speaking about Nero?

Is the whole world yet to experience seven years of untold misery in what is termed the Great Tribulation, or have the events described in Revelation already taken place in and to the nation of Israel between AD 64-70? Is there to be a literal one thousand year reign of Jesus on the physical earth from the literal throne of David in Jerusalem, or did that event take place between His ascension in AD 30 to His glorious return in AD 70? Did not Peter tell the Jews that Jesus assumed David's throne when God raised Him from the dead? He said,

"Men and brethren, let me freely speak unto you of the patriarch David, that he is both dead and buried, and his sepulchre is with us unto this day. Therefore being a prophet, and knowing that God had sworn with an oath to him, that of the fruit of his loins, according to the flesh, he would raise up Christ to sit on his throne; He seeing this before spake of the resurrection of Christ, that his soul was not left in hell, neither his flesh did see corruption. This Jesus hath God raised up, whereof we all are witnesses. Therefore being by the right hand of God exalted, and having received of the Father the promise of the Holy Ghost, he hath shed forth this, which ye now see and hear. For David is not ascended into the heavens: but he saith himself, The LORD said unto my Lord, Sit thou on my right hand, Until I make thy foes thy footstool. Therefore let all the house of Israel know assuredly, that God hath made that same Jesus, whom ye have crucified, both Lord and Christ." Acts 2:29-36

Is there to be a literal resurrection of physical bodies and a judgment passed upon on all men, or did Jesus raise the dead and pass judgment when He returned in AD 70? Jesus said while He was still alive,

"Verily, verily, I say unto you, He that heareth my word, and believeth on him that sent me, hath everlasting life, and shall not come into condemnation (judgment); but is passed from death unto life. Verily, verily, I say unto you, The hour is coming, and now is, when the dead shall hear the voice of the Son of God: and they that hear shall live. For as the Father hath life in himself; so hath he given to the Son to have life in himself; And hath given him authority to execute judgment also, because he is the Son of man. Marvel not at this: for the hour is coming, in the which all that are in the graves shall hear his voice, And shall come forth; they that have done good, unto the resurrection of life; and they that have done evil, unto the resurrection of damnation.

I can of mine own self do nothing: as I hear, I judge: and my judgment is just; because I seek not mine own will, but the will of the Father which hath sent me." John 5:24-30

Is this world about to be destroyed, or was God telling the truth when He said it was made to abide forever?

"One generation passeth away, and another generation cometh: but the earth abideth for ever." Ecclesiastes 1:4

"Who laid the foundations of the earth, that it should not be removed for ever." Psalm 104:5

"Thy faithfulness is unto all generations: thou hast established the earth, and it abideth" Psalm 119:90

WHAT DOES SHORTLY MEAN?

To me the key to all these questions and the solutions to all the problems lies in two verses, one in Chapter 1 the other in Chapter 22. The very first verse of the Revelation says,

*"The Revelation of Jesus Christ, which God gave unto him, to shew unto his servants things which **must shortly come to pass**; and he sent and signified it by his angel unto his servant John:" Revelation 1:1*

In the final chapter John said,

*"And he (Jesus) said unto me, These sayings are faithful and true: and the Lord God of the holy prophets sent his angel to shew unto his servants **the things which must shortly be done.**" Revelation 22:6*

The key is the definition of the word "shortly." The English word "shortly" is found fifteen times in the King James version of the Bible. In the dictionary it is defined as, *"in a little time."* The word is found three times in the Old Testament and twelve times in the New Testament. Every time it is used it refers to something that is to take place in a short period of time. Never does it mean that when the event does occur it will occur quickly or rapidly. It always deals with a brief period of time. For example, the first time we find it used is when Joseph interpreted Pharaoh's dream and said,

> *"And for that the dream was doubled unto Pharaoh twice; it is because the thing is established by God, and God will **shortly** bring it to pass." Genesis 41:32*

In the New Testament the first occurrence is when Paul was before Festus and some of the Jews urged him to send him to Jerusalem having laid a plot to kill Paul,

> *"But Festus answered, that Paul should be kept at Caesarea, and that he himself would depart **shortly** thither." Acts 25:4*

Would one logically assume that Festus meant that when he did take action that he would depart it quickly? No, rather they would think that he would depart in a brief period of time.

If we examine the other eleven times the world "shortly" is used, we will find it is used in the same sense. So why should we think the two times it is found in the Revelation it means something different? What Jesus said was that the events described in the Revelation were to take place in a very short period of time. This agrees with what Jesus stated in the Olivet discourse when He said,

> *"Verily I say unto you, This generation shall not pass, till all these things be fulfilled." Matthew 24:34*

It is my opinion that Revelation is John's version of Matthew 24, Mark 13 and Luke 21-22. All these things were to come upon Israel as punishment for their sin of rejecting Him as the Messiah. John said,

> *"He came unto his own, and his own received him not." John 1:11*

Jesus said to the leader in Israel,

> *"Ye serpents, ye generation of vipers, how can ye escape the damnation of hell? Wherefore, behold, I send unto you prophets, and wise men, and scribes: and some of them ye shall kill and crucify; and some of them shall ye scourge in your synagogues, and persecute them from city to city: That upon you may come all the righteous blood shed upon the earth, from the blood of righteous Abel unto the blood of Zacharias son of Barachias, whom ye slew between the temple and the altar. Verily I say unto you, **All these things shall come upon this generation.** O Jerusalem, Jerusalem, thou that killest the prophets, and stonest them which are sent unto thee, how often would I have gathered thy children together, even as a hen gathereth her chickens under her wings, and ye would not! Behold, your house is left unto you desolate. For I say unto you, Ye shall not see me henceforth, till ye shall say, Blessed is he that cometh in the name of the Lord." Matthew 23:33-39*

CHAPTER I

JUST TAKE HIM AT HIS WORD

Instead of trying to push the events described in Revelation into some distant date from the time they were given, why not just take Jesus and the apostles at their word and understand that He was showing things that were to take place soon from that day, and not our day? To lift an event from the time intended and push it into a future time not intended is to be guilty of an anachronism, that is assigning an event to a time not intended.

Jesus told his disciples that some of them would live to see Him coming in His kingdom. He said,

> *"For the Son of man shall come in the glory of his Father with his angels; and then he shall reward every man according to his works. Verily I say unto you, There be some standing here, which shall not taste of death, till they see the Son of man coming in his kingdom."* Matthew 16:27-28

Paul certainly believed that Jesus was coming soon for He said to the suffering saints in Thessalonica,

> *"But I would not have you to be ignorant, brethren, concerning them which are asleep, that ye sorrow not, even as others which have no hope. For if we believe that Jesus died and rose again, even so them also which sleep in Jesus will God bring with him. For this we say unto you by the word of the Lord, that **we which are alive and remain unto the coming of the Lord** shall not prevent them which are asleep. For the Lord*

*himself shall descend from heaven with a shout, with the voice of the archangel, and with the trump of God: and the dead in Christ shall rise first: Then we which are alive and remain shall be caught up together with them in the clouds, to meet the Lord in the air: and so shall we ever be with the Lord. **Wherefore comfort one another with these words**." I Thessalonians 4:13-18*

What is there comforting to first century believers who were suffering if the events Paul spoke of were not to take place for hundreds or even thousands of years? Nothing, the events described by Paul were imminent, if that were to soon unfold.

The writer to the Hebrews believed that Jesus would come soon from his day, not our day. He said,

*"Cast not away therefore your confidence, which hath great recompence of reward. For ye have need of patience, that, after ye have done the will of God, ye might receive the promise. **For yet a little while, and he that shall come will come, and will not tarry**. Now the just shall live by faith: but if any man draw back, my soul shall have no pleasure in him. But we are not of them who draw back unto perdition; but of them that believe to the saving of the soul." Hebrews 10:35-39*

James was expecting Jesus to return for he said,

*"Be patient therefore, brethren, unto the coming of the Lord. Behold, the husbandman waiteth for the precious fruit of the earth, and hath long patience for it, until he receive the early and latter rain. Be ye also patient; stablish your hearts: for **the coming of the Lord draweth nigh.** Grudge not one against another, brethren, lest ye be condemned: behold, the judge standeth before the door." James 5:7-9*

THE PAROUSIA

The primary Greek word translated "coming" is "*parousia*" and means "arrival" or "presence." Jesus linked and time limited His "*parousia*" with the destruction of Jerusalem, the Jewish temple and the end of the Old covenant age. Never does the word "second" appear before the word "coming" in the New Testament. The term "second coming" like the word "rapture" is inserted by men.

When Paul said that,

> *"we which are alive and remain unto the **coming** of the Lord" he used the word "Parousia."*

When James said,

> *"the **coming** of the Lord draweth nigh"*

he used the word the word "*Parousia.*" And many other examples can be cited where, when speaking of the coming of the Lord, this same word was used.

If Jesus did not return when He said He would then we are still living under the law and are still waiting for the salvation Peter said was to be revealed in the last time. He said to the men of his day,

> *"Blessed be the God and Father of our Lord Jesus Christ, which according to his abundant mercy hath begotten us again unto a lively hope by the resurrection of Jesus Christ from the dead, To an inheritance incorruptible, and undefiled, and that fadeth not away, reserved in heaven for you, Who are kept by the power of God through faith unto salvation ready to be revealed*

in the last time. Wherein ye greatly rejoice, though now for a season, if need be, ye are in heaviness through manifold temptations: That the trial of your faith, being much more precious than of gold that perisheth, though it be tried with fire, might be found unto praise and honour and glory at the appearing of Jesus Christ: Whom having not seen, ye love; in whom, though now ye see him not, yet believing, ye rejoice with joy unspeakable and full of glory: Receiving the end of your faith, even the salvation of your souls." I Peter 1:3-9

If Jesus has not returned as promised then the souls of those who died in faith under the Old Covenant have not yet been released from captivity and when we die we too will have to go into that holding place called Sheol and wait until He comes and raises us and all others out of that place.

But if He did come when He said He would, those who patiently waited were released from Sheol and were taken to heaven after He entered the true Holy place and secured eternal redemption for His elect. The writer to the Hebrews tells us that those who waited in Sheol were made perfect or complete when Jesus finished the work of securing eternal redemption. He said of them,

"These all died in faith, not having received the promises, but having seen them afar off, and were persuaded of them, and embraced them, and confessed that they were strangers and pilgrims on the earth. For they that say such things declare plainly that they seek a country. And truly, if they had been mindful of that country from whence they came out, they might have had opportunity to have returned. But now they desire a better country, that is, an heavenly: wherefore

God is not ashamed to be called their God: for he hath prepared for them a city." Hebrews 11:13-16

And then he said,

"They were stoned, they were sawn asunder, were tempted, were slain with the sword: they wandered about in sheepskins and goatskins; being destitute, afflicted, tormented; (Of whom the world was not worthy:) they wandered in deserts, and in mountains, and in dens and caves of the earth. And these all, having obtained a good report through faith, received not the promise: God having provided some better thing for us, that they without us should not be made perfect [complete]." Hebrews 11:37-40

WHAT DID JESUS DO WHILE HIS BODY LAY IN JOSEPH'S TOMB

Paul describes what Jesus did in His Spirit during those three days while His body lay in Joseph's new tomb. He said,

"Wherefore he saith, When he ascended up on high, he led captivity captive, and gave gifts unto men. (Now that he ascended, what is it but that he also descended first into the lower parts of the earth? He that descended is the same also that ascended up far above all heavens, that he might fill [fulfill] all things." Ephesians 4:8-10

Peter explained it with these words,

"For Christ also hath once suffered for sins, the just for the unjust, that he might bring us to God, being put to death in the flesh, but quickened by the Spirit: By which also he went and preached unto the spirits in prison; Which sometime were disobedient, when once the

longsuffering of God waited in the days of Noah, while the ark was a preparing, wherein few, that is, eight souls were saved by water." I Peter 3:18-20

PREDICTED IN THE OLD TESTAMENT

This glorious event was predicted by several of the writers of the Old Testament. God said to Hosea,

"I will ransom them from the power of the grave; I will redeem them from death: O death, I will be thy plagues; O grave, I will be thy destruction: repentance shall be hid from mine eyes." Hosea 13:14

Job anticipated it for he said,

"For I know that my redeemer liveth, and that he shall stand at the latter day upon the earth: And though after my skin worms destroy this body, yet in my flesh shall I see God: Whom I shall see for myself, and mine eyes shall behold, and not another; though my reins be consumed within me." Job 19:25-27

Daniel was promised participation in it, for God said to him,

"And many of them that sleep in the dust of the earth shall awake, some to everlasting life, and some to shame and everlasting contempt." Daniel 12:2

"But go thou thy way till the end be: for thou shalt rest, and stand in thy lot at the end of the days." Daniel 12:13

David believed that he would experience resurrection for he said,

"As for me, I will behold thy face in righteousness: I shall be satisfied, when I awake, with thy likeness." Psalm 17:15

This agrees with what John said,

"Beloved, now are we the sons of God, and it doth not yet appear what we shall be: but we know that, when he shall appear, we shall be like him; for we shall see him as he is." I John 3:2

EXPECTED BY THE WRITERS OF THE NEW TESTAMENT

John records what Jesus said about it when he wrote,

*"Verily, verily, I say unto you, He that heareth my word, and believeth on him that sent me, hath everlasting life, and shall not come into condemnation; but is passed from death unto life. Verily, verily, I say unto you, The hour is coming, **and now is**, when the dead shall hear the voice of the Son of God: and they that hear shall live. For as the Father hath life in himself; so hath he given to the Son to have life in himself; And hath given him authority to execute judgment also, because he is the Son of man. Marvel not at this: for the hour is coming, in the which all that are in the graves shall hear his voice, And shall come forth; they that have done good, unto the resurrection of life; and they that have done evil, unto the resurrection of damnation." John 5:24-29*

Jesus also affirmed to Martha when He said,

"Thy brother shall rise again. Martha saith unto him, I know that he shall rise again in the resurrection at the last day. Jesus said unto her, I am the resurrection, and the life: he that believeth in me, though he were dead,

yet shall he live: And whosoever liveth and believeth in me shall never die. Believest thou this?" John 11:23-26

What did Jesus mean when He said,

"I am the resurrection and the life?"

He meant that those who died before He secured eternal redemption were in need of resurrection, but all those who were saved after He had finished His task no longer needed resurrection for they have eternal life. After He,

"by his own blood he entered in once into the holy place, having obtained eternal redemption for us. For if the blood of bulls and of goats, and the ashes of an heifer sprinkling the unclean, sanctifieth to the purifying of the flesh:" Hebrews 9:12-13

It is now as John said,

"And I heard a voice from heaven saying unto me, Write, Blessed are the dead which die in the Lord from henceforth: Yea, saith the Spirit, that they may rest from their labours; and their works do follow them." Revelation 14:13

A great change took place when Jesus finished the work of redemption. Now it is straight to heaven for all who die in the Lord, no more waiting in Sheol. Paul said,

"For we know that if our earthly house of this tabernacle were dissolved, we have a building of God, an house not made with hands, eternal in the heavens. For in this we groan, earnestly desiring to be clothed upon with our house which is from heaven: If so be that being clothed we shall not be found naked. For we that are in this tabernacle do groan, being burdened: not for that we would be unclothed, but clothed upon, that mortality might be swallowed up of life. Now he that hath wrought us for the selfsame thing is God, who also hath given

unto us the earnest of the Spirit. Therefore we are always confident, knowing that, whilst we are at home in the body, we are absent from the Lord: (For we walk by faith, not by sight:) We are confident, I say, and willing rather to be absent from the body, and to be present with the Lord." II Corinthians 5:1-8

CHAPTER II

WHEN WAS RESURRECTION COMPLETED?

Paul nails it down as to time when he said,

"If in this life only we have hope in Christ, we are of all men most miserable. But now is Christ risen from the dead, and become the firstfruits of them that slept. For since by man came death, by man came also the resurrection of the dead. For as in Adam all die, even so in Christ shall all be made alive. But every man in his own order: Christ the firstfruits; afterward they that are Christ's at his coming (parousia). Then cometh the end, when he shall have delivered up the kingdom to God, even the Father; when he shall have put down all rule and all authority and power. For he must reign, till he hath put all enemies under his feet. The last enemy that shall be destroyed is death." I Corinthians 15:19-26

When Paul stood before Agrippa and said,

"Whereupon, O king Agrippa, I was not disobedient unto the heavenly vision: But shewed first unto them of Damascus, and at Jerusalem, and throughout all the coasts of Judaea, and then to the Gentiles, that they should repent and turn to God, and do works meet for repentance. For these causes the Jews caught me in the temple, and went about to kill me. Having therefore obtained help of God, I continue unto this day, witnessing both to small and great, saying none other things than those which the prophets and Moses did say should come: That Christ should suffer, and that he should be the first that should rise from the dead, and should shew light unto the people, and to the Gentiles." Acts 26:19-23

When Paul said,

> *"that Christ should suffer, and be the first that should rise from the dead, and should show light unto the people, and to the Gentiles"*

he used the Greek word *"mello"* which literally means, *"about to be."*

This same Greek word was used by Paul when he said to the men in Athens,

> *"And the times of this ignorance God winked at; but now commandeth all men every where to repent: Because he hath appointed a day, in the which he will judge the world in righteousness by that man whom he hath ordained; whereof he hath given assurance unto all men, in that he hath raised him from the dead." Acts 17:30-31*

All of these great events; the return of Jesus, the resurrection of the dead and the judgment were to all take place shortly. To push them into the distant future is to destroy the clear meaning of words and render them useless to those to whom they were written. What possible comfort would the Thessalonians have found in the words spoken by Paul if what he was talking about was not to occur for hundreds of years? What he was telling them, they were about to experience.

THE IMPORTANCE OF GETTING IT RIGHT

Some people say one's view of eschatology does not matter. But how one understands the events described in Revelation is life changing. If the futurists are correct and we are living in the last days on a dying planet, what incentive does one have to try to improve the things around them? There is no hope, except what they call the hope of Jesus' return to destroy this planet and create a new one. But if God meant what He said to Noah then we need to be working to preserve this planet and spread the message of Jesus to everyone. We are not sailing on a sinking ship. We are living in the world that God said would never again be destroyed. He said to Noah,

*"I will not again curse the ground any more for man's sake; for the imagination of man's heart is evil from his youth; neither will I again smite any more every thing living, as I have done. While the earth remaineth, seedtime and harvest, and cold and heat, and summer and winter, and day and night **shall not cease.**" Genesis 8:21-11*

And then God said,

*"And I will establish my covenant with you; neither shall all flesh be cut off any more by the waters of a flood; neither shall there any more be a flood to destroy the earth. And God said, This is the token of the covenant which I make between me and you and every living creature that is with you, for **perpetual generations:** I do set my bow in the cloud, and it shall be for a token of a covenant between me and the earth. And it shall come to pass, when I bring a cloud over the earth, that the bow shall be seen in the cloud: And I will remember my covenant, which is between me and you and every living creature of all flesh; and the waters shall no more become a flood to destroy all flesh. And the bow shall be in the cloud; and I will look upon it, that I may remember the everlasting covenant between God and*

every living creature of all flesh that is upon the earth."
Genesis 9:11-16

WE NOW LIVE IN THE AGES TO COME

When Paul wrote to the Ephesians he spoke of, *"ages to come."* He said,

> *"Even when we were dead in sins, hath quickened us together with Christ, (by grace ye are saved;) And hath raised us up together, and made us sit together in heavenly places in Christ Jesus: That in the ages to come he might shew the exceeding riches of his grace in his kindness toward us through Christ Jesus. For by grace are ye saved through faith; and that not of yourselves: it is the gift of God: Not of works, lest any man should boast. For we are his workmanship, created in Christ Jesus unto good works, which God hath before ordained that we should walk in them"* Ephesians 2:5-10

What was future for him is now reality for us. He also spoke to Titus of something great that was still future for him but is now history for us. He said,

> *"For the grace of God that bringeth salvation hath appeared to all men, Teaching us that, denying ungodliness and worldly lusts, we should live soberly, righteously, and godly, in this present world; Looking for that blessed hope, and the glorious appearing of the great God and our Saviour Jesus Christ; Who gave himself for us, that he might redeem us from all iniquity, and purify unto himself a peculiar people, zealous of good works."* Titus 2:11-14

This was something Paul was looking for in his day, not something that Christians should still be looking for today. What was a *"blessed hope"* for his generation is the *"glorious heritage"* for our generation. Paul said,

> *"For we are saved by hope: but hope that is seen is not hope: for what a man seeth, why doth he yet hope for?" Romans 8:24*

Believers before AD 70 lived in hope, since Jesus' return believers live in confidence. Solomon said,

> *"Hope deferred maketh the heart sick: but when the desire cometh, it is a tree of life." Proverbs 13:12*

Because He has returned, we live to serve Him until we die and then be received into the place that He has prepared for us. The writer to the Hebrews was confident of this for he said to the men of his day,

> *"Cast not away therefore your confidence, which hath great recompence of reward. For ye have need of patience, that, after ye have done the will of God, ye might receive the promise. **For yet a little while, and he that shall come will come, and will not tarry.** Now the just shall live by faith: but if any man draw back, my soul shall have no pleasure in him. But we are not of them who draw back unto perdition; but of them that believe to the saving of the soul." Hebrews 10:35-39*

CHAPTER III

WHAT DOES REVELATION SHOW?

Some say Revelation describes the horrors that are coming on the whole world. That it tells us that great tribulation is coming our way. They say that everything will eventually be destroyed and Jesus will make all things new. But if He returned when and as He said He would and the things written in this letter concerned the nation of Israel and the judgment of God upon her for her rejection of Jesus as the Messiah, then everything recorded in this book is history and we are living in the eternal age.

When John says that these things came upon the earth he used the Greek word *"ge."* For example he said,

> *"The first angel sounded, and there followed hail and fire mingled with blood, and they were cast upon the **earth**: and the third part of trees was burnt up, and all green grass was burnt up." Revelation 8:7*

In most instances *"ge"* refers to the land of Israel, not the entire global world.

Those judgments came upon Israel during the time of great tribulation between AD 64-70. Jesus spoke of this in the Olivet discourse. He said,

> *"For then shall be great tribulation, such as was not since the beginning of the world to this time, no, nor ever shall be. And except those days should be shortened, there should no flesh be saved: but for the*

elect's sake those days shall be shortened." Matthew 24:21-22

He went on to say,

"Verily I say unto you, This generation shall not pass, till all these things be fulfilled." Matthew 24:34

Luke tells us that Jesus told His people to flee when they saw these things coming. He said,

*"And when ye shall see Jerusalem compassed with armies, then know that the desolation thereof is nigh. Then let them which are in Judaea flee to the mountains; and let them which are in the midst of it depart out; and let not them that are in the countries enter thereinto. For these be the days of vengeance, that **all things which are written may be fulfilled.**" Luke 21:20-22*

History tells us that all believers in Jerusalem fled to the little city of Pella before the city was destroyed and not a single life was lost. God preserved them just as Jesus said He would. These words describe what happened during the invasion of the Roman army on Jerusalem. They have nothing to do with events that are to take place in the so called "last days" of planet earth.

Jesus emphasized the nearness of the unfolding of the events described in this book when He said,

*"Blessed is he that readeth, and they that hear the words of this prophecy, and keep those things which are written therein: for **the time is at hand.**" Revelation 1:3*

He further time limited it when He said,

> *"Behold, he cometh with clouds; and every eye shall see him, and they also which pierced him: and all kindreds of the earth shall wail because of him. Even so, Amen." Revelation 1:7*

The coming in the clouds is an Old Testament figure of the coming of the Lord in judgment on sinful people. The expression, *"every eye shall see him,"* is just another way of saying that men will be aware of His return in judgment. If those who pierced Him were to be living at the time of His return it had to be somewhere close to AD 70. Those who nailed Him to the cross were probably men about His age when he was crucified, so they would have been in their seventies when He returned.

These messages were sent to seven actual churches that existed when John received the Revelation, not to us today. The Bible as a whole was written for us but not to us. If we fail to understand audience relevance we will greatly err in our interpretation of Scripture.

WHAT DID JOHN SEE?

When Jesus had finished dictating the seven letters to the seven church He said to John,

> *"Come up hither, and I will shew thee things which must be hereafter." Revelation 4:1*

Thus, began an exciting and amazing revelation as Jesus showed John what was about to happen in Israel. The very things that had been shown to Daniel, but had been ordered sealed, up were about to be revealed.

Recognizing that highly figurative language is used in the book is the key to understanding its message. When Jesus spoke of twenty-four elders he was using symbolic language to describe the saved of all ages, both from the Jews under the Old covenant and the Gentiles, under the New covenant. The same number and symbol is used in the description of the New Jerusalem, the church, the Lamb's wife. Note what John said about that city,

*"And he carried me away in the spirit to a great and high mountain, and shewed me that great city, the holy Jerusalem, descending out of heaven from God, Having the glory of God: and her light was like unto a stone most precious, even like a jasper stone, clear as crystal; And had a wall great and high, and had twelve gates, and at the gates twelve angels, and names written thereon, which are **the names of the twelve tribes of the children of Israel**: On the east three gates; on the north three gates; on the south three gates; and on the west three gates. And the wall of the city had twelve foundations, and in them **the names of the twelve apostles of the Lamb.**" Revelation 21:10-14*

THE TWO BROUGHT TOGETHER

This is what Jesus said He was going to do. He said ,

"I am the good shepherd, and know my sheep, and am known of mine. As the Father knoweth me, even so know I the Father: and I lay down my life for the sheep. And other sheep I have, which are not of this fold: them

*also I must bring, and they shall hear my voice; and **there shall be one fold, and one shepherd.*** *" John 10:14-16*

Paul explained how He did this when he said to the Gentiles at the church at Ephesus,

*"Wherefore remember, that ye being in time past Gentiles in the flesh, who are called Uncircumcision by that which is called the Circumcision in the flesh made by hands; That at that time ye were without Christ, being aliens from the commonwealth of Israel, and strangers from the covenants of promise, having no hope, and without God in the world: But now in Christ Jesus ye who sometimes were far off are made nigh by the blood of Christ. For he is our peace, **who hath made both one**, and hath broken down the middle wall of partition between us; Having abolished in his flesh the enmity, even the law of commandments contained in ordinances; for to make in himself of twain one new man, so making peace; And that he might reconcile both unto God in one body by the cross, having slain the enmity thereby: And came and preached peace to you which were afar off, and to them that were nigh. For through him we both have access by one Spirit unto the Father. Now therefore ye are no more strangers and foreigners, but fellowcitizens with the saints, and of the household of God; And are built upon the foundation of the apostles and prophets, Jesus Christ himself being the chief corner stone; In whom all the building fitly framed together groweth unto an holy temple in the Lord: In whom ye also are builded together for an habitation of God through the Spirit." Ephesians 2:11-22*

ALL THE SAVED ARE IN THAT ONE BODY

Under the Old covenant the Gentiles were largely excluded from the kingdom, but when Israel broke their covenant with God the kingdom was taken from them and given to a new nation. Jesus said to His infant church,

"Fear not, little flock; for it is your Father's good pleasure to give you the kingdom." Luke 12:32

Paul elaborated on this when he said,

*"In whom (Jesus) we have redemption through his blood, even the forgiveness of sins: Who is the image of the invisible God, the firstborn of every creature: For by him were all things created, that are in heaven, and that are in earth, visible and invisible, whether they be thrones, or dominions, or principalities, or powers: all things were created by him, and for him: And he is before all things, and by him all things consist. **And he is the head of the body, the church**: who is the beginning, the firstborn from the dead; that in all things he might have the preeminence. For it pleased the Father that in him should all fulness dwell; And, having made peace through the blood of his cross, by him to reconcile all things unto himself; by him, I say, whether they be things in earth, or things in heaven. And you, that were sometime alienated and enemies in your mind by wicked works, yet now hath he reconciled In the body of his flesh through death, to present you holy and unblameable and unreproveable in his sight: If ye continue in the faith grounded and settled, and be not moved away from the hope of the gospel, which ye have heard, and which was preached to every creature which is under heaven; whereof I Paul am made a minister; Who now rejoice in my sufferings for you, and fill up that which is behind of the afflictions of Christ in my flesh for **his body's sake, which is the church**: Whereof I am made a minister, according to the dispensation of God which is given to me for you, to*

> *fulfil the word of God; Even the mystery which hath been hid from ages and from generations, but now is made manifest to his saints: To whom God would make known what is the riches of the glory of this mystery among the Gentiles; which is Christ in you, the hope of glory:" Colossians 1:14-27*

In Jesus, both Jews and Gentiles are in one body, that is His church. The church exists in two realms, the visible, those of us who are still on the earth in fleshly bodies, and the invisible, those who have died and have received a new body fashioned like unto His glorious body.

ISRAEL LEFT DESOLATE

Due to her sins and the rejection of Jesus, the nation of Israel was left desolate and the church was married to the Lord Jesus and she is His wife. The mystery that had been baffling men for generations was solved when both Jew and Gentile were brought into one body, the church. Paul said,

> *"If ye have heard of the dispensation of the grace of God which is given me to you-ward: How that by revelation he made known unto me the mystery; (as I wrote afore in few words, Whereby, when ye read, ye may understand my knowledge in the mystery of Christ) Which in other ages was not made known unto the sons of men, as it is now revealed unto his holy apostles and prophets by the Spirit;* ***That the Gentiles should be fellowheirs, and of the same body, and partakers of his promise in Christ by the gospel:*** *Whereof I was made a minister, according to the gift of the grace of God given unto me by the effectual working of his power. Unto me, who am less than the least of all saints, is this grace given, that I should preach among the*

Gentiles the unsearchable riches of Christ; And to make all men see what is the fellowship of the mystery, which from the beginning of the world hath been hid in God, who created all things by Jesus Christ: To the intent that now unto the principalities and powers in heavenly places might be known by the church the manifold wisdom of God, According to the eternal purpose which he purposed in Christ Jesus our Lord: In whom we have boldness and access with confidence by the faith of him." Ephesians 3:2-12

ACCORDING TO THE ETERNAL PURPOSE

It was no accident or second thought with God that Jews and Gentiles were brought into one body. Only when we understand that God decreed from the beginning what should be, will we understand the message of the Bible, especially that of Revelation. What God has purposed will be, for Isaiah said about the demise of Assyria,

> *"The LORD of hosts hath sworn, saying, Surely as I have thought, so shall it come to pass; and as **I have purposed, so shall it stand:**" Isaiah 14:24*

God raised up the nation of Israel to be His special people and entered into a covenant with them, but it was a conditional covenant. He said if they would keep His covenant then He would bless them, but if they broke the covenant He would bring a curse upon them. God said to Israel,

> *"See, I have set before thee this day life and good, and death and evil; In that I command thee this day to love the LORD thy God, to walk in his ways, and to keep his*

commandments and his statutes and his judgments, that thou mayest live and multiply: and the LORD thy God shall bless thee in the land whither thou goest to possess it." Deuteronomy 30:15-16

But then He said,

"But if thine heart turn away, so that thou wilt not hear, but shalt be drawn away, and worship other gods, and serve them; I denounce unto you this day, that ye shall surely perish, and that ye shall not prolong your days upon the land, whither thou passest over Jordan to go to possess it." Deuteronomy 30:17-18

When they broke the covenant, God divorced Israel. Jeremiah said,

"And I saw, when for all the causes whereby backsliding Israel committed adultery I had put her away, and given her a bill of divorce; yet her treacherous sister Judah feared not, but went and played the harlot also." Jeremiah 3:8

We know that Israel was the nation through whom the Messiah was to come, but when He came, as a nation, they rejected Jesus and called for His crucifixion. For this reason, Israel was rejected and the church was chosen to be the bride of Christ. The book of Revelation is the record of how Israel was rejected and the church, the New Jerusalem, was revealed as the bride of Jesus Christ. John said,

"And I John saw the holy city, new Jerusalem, coming down from God out of heaven, prepared as a bride adorned for her husband." Revelation 21:2

And then he said,

"And there came unto me one of the seven angels which had the seven vials full of the seven last plagues, and talked with me, saying, Come hither, I will shew thee the bride, the Lamb's wife." Revelation 21:9

THE GENTILES BROUGHT IN

When Jesus came into the world He came only to the lost sheep of the house of Israel. He said to woman of Canaan who came to Him asking for mercy,

"I am not sent but unto the lost sheep of the house of Israel." Matthew 15:24

When He sent the apostles out two by two He said,

"But go rather to the lost sheep of the house of Israel." Matthew 10:6

But when He spoke to the Jews about being the great shepherd He said,

"other sheep I have, which are not of this fold: them also I must bring, and they shall hear my voice; and there shall be one fold, and one shepherd." John 10:16

When the Jews pressed Jesus as to whether or not He was the Christ, Jesus answered them,

"I told you, and ye believed not: the works that I do in my Father's name, they bear witness of me. But ye believe not, because ye are not of my sheep, as I said unto you." John 10:25-26

WHY DID THE JEWS REJECT JESUS?

The answer is simple, He did not match the profile they had about the coming Messiah. They were expecting a Messiah who would restore to them the kingdom as it had been in the days of David and Solomon. When He did not lead them against Rome and restore a physical kingdom, they rejected Him. Even His close associates held this view of His kingdom. After He had risen from the dead He joined two disciples on the road to Emmaus but they did not recognize Him,

> *"And he said unto them, What manner of communications are these that ye have one to another, as ye walk, and are sad? And the one of them, whose name was Cleopas, answering said unto him, Art thou only a stranger in Jerusalem, and hast not known the things which are come to pass there in these days? And he said unto them, What things? And they said unto him, Concerning Jesus of Nazareth, which was a prophet mighty in deed and word before God and all the people: And how the chief priests and our rulers delivered him to be condemned to death, and have crucified him. But **we trusted that it had been he which should have redeemed Israel**: and beside all this, to day is the third day since these things were done." Luke 24:17-21*

Even after He explained to them how He had to suffer and enter into His glory or kingdom they still did not understand, for just before He ascended back to the Father they asked,

> *"Lord, wilt thou at this time restore again the kingdom to Israel? And he said unto them, It is not for you to know the times or the seasons, which the Father hath put in his own power." Acts 1:6-7*

This was in spite of the fact that He had said,

"My kingdom is not of this world: if my kingdom were of this world, then would my servants fight, that I should not be delivered to the Jews: but now is my kingdom not from hence." John 18:36

He had made it clear that His kingdom was spiritual and not material,

"And when he was demanded of the Pharisees, when the kingdom of God should come, he answered them and said, The kingdom of God cometh not with observation: Neither shall they say, Lo here! or, lo there! for, behold, the kingdom of God is within you [within you: or, among you]." Luke 17:20-21

But an even stranger thing to me is that my futurist friends are still waiting for Him to return and set up a material kingdom on the earth. This despite the fact that when the seventh trumpet sounded,

"there were great voices in heaven, saying, The kingdoms of this world are become the kingdoms of our Lord, and of his Christ; and he shall reign for ever and ever." Revelation 11:15

THE APOSTLE TO THE GENTILES

Paul was called to be the apostle to the Gentiles, but in the beginning of his ministry he always went first to the Jews. When he visited Antioch, Luke says he went to the synagogue and communed with the Jews. As he spoke, Gentiles also came to hear him,

"But when the Jews saw the multitudes, they were filled with envy, and spake against those things which were

FORTY YEARS TO REPENT

When Jesus died on the cross the veil of the temple was rent in half, signifying that the way to God was now open to all people of all nations who would come. But for the next forty years the Jews continued to practice Judaism and failed to accept Jesus as the Messiah. As He has always done, God gave them time to repent, but they repented not, so judgment came upon that nation in AD 70 when the Roman army marched against Jerusalem and destroyed the city, the temple and all genealogical records so no man could serve as a priest again. On that day Biblical Judaism died. The Old covenant age ended.

What Jesus said came true. He said,

would not! Behold, your house is left unto you desolate."
Matthew 23:37-38

This all came to a head when Jesus returned, not in a literal body, but in judgment upon Israel and gave the kingdom to the church.

This is the return He promised and the one all the writing Apostles were expecting. It came on time in just the way He said it would. Paul describes the devastation brought when Jesus returned and gave assurance to the saints in Thessalonica that they would be revenged on their enemies. He said,

> *"Seeing it is a righteous thing with God to recompense tribulation to them that trouble you; And to you who are troubled rest with us, when the Lord Jesus shall be revealed from heaven with his mighty angels, In flaming fire taking vengeance on them that know not God, and that obey not the gospel of our Lord Jesus Christ: Who shall be punished with everlasting destruction from the presence of the Lord, and from the glory of his power; When he shall come to be glorified in his saints, and to be admired in all them that believe (because our testimony among you was believed) in that day. Wherefore also we pray always for you, that our God would count you worthy of this calling, and fulfil all the good pleasure of his goodness, and the work of faith with power:" II Thessalonians 1:6-11*

THIS IS WHAT REVELATION DESCRIBES

What Paul said here is exactly what took place in Israel in AD 70 and it is what the Revelation is all about. It is the record of God's judgment upon Israel. To lift it out of this context and apply it to another time and place is to wrest the scriptures. When you read the book with this mind set it makes perfect sense. In his writings Josephus, a first century Jew who was a diplomat, a general and an historian, details just what happened when the Romans invaded and destroyed Jerusalem. To learn more about this secure a copy of his works and read for yourself.

That which had been shown to Daniel many years earlier was to be unfolded as Jesus took the sealed book opened it and revealed what was therein. When God showed it to Daniel he said,

> *"Then I Daniel looked, and, behold, there stood other two, the one on this side of the bank of the river, and the other on that side of the bank of the river. And one said to the man clothed in linen, which was upon the waters of the river, How long shall it be to the end of these wonders? And I heard the man clothed in linen, which was upon the waters of the river, when he held up his right hand and his left hand unto heaven, and sware by him that liveth for ever that it shall be for a time, times, and an half; and when he shall have accomplished to scatter the power of the holy people, all these things shall be finished. And I heard, but I understood not: then said I, O my Lord, what shall be the end of these things? And he said, Go thy way, Daniel: for the words are closed up and sealed till the time of the end." Daniel 12:5-9*

THE TIME OF THE END

This was to be revealed at the time of the end. The end of the nation of Israel. This is the meaning of the last days, the end of the world (age), the last hour and the day of the Lord. The things predicted in the Revelation took place at the end of the Jewish age, when the power of the holy people was broken. It all centers in the life and ministry of Jesus. History revolves around the life of Jesus. It is that day spoken of by David when he said,

> *"The stone which the builders refused is become the head stone of the corner. This is the LORD'S doing; it is marvellous in our eyes. This is the day which the LORD hath made; we will rejoice and be glad in it." Psalm 118:22-24*

This is not a reference to just any twenty-four hour day, it refers to the fulfillment of the day of Christ. The time He spent on this earth to secure eternal redemption for His lost sheep. Jesus said that to the unbelieving Jews,

> *"Your father Abraham rejoiced to see my day: and he saw it, and was glad." John 8:56*

There are three dates included in the day of the Lord. In our next chapter we will review each of them.

CHAPTER IV

THE MOST IMPORTANT THREE DAYS OF HISTORY

When David wrote,

> *"This is the day which the LORD hath made; we will rejoice and be glad in it." Psalm 118:24*

he was not talking about just a twenty four hour time period that we call a day. He used the word "day" to speak of that time when God sent His Son into the world to secure eternal redemption for His lost people.

This covers the time from the day Jesus was born of the virgin to the time when He died on the cross, was buried, was raised from the dead, ascended back into heaven and returned in power and glory in judgment upon Israel. The date runs from BC 4 to AD 70. If one fails to understand the significance of each of these days, he will not understand God's purpose in becoming a man in the person of Jesus Christ.

THESE DAYS WERE FORESEEN

The first reference to the purpose for these days is found in Genesis 3:15 when God said to the serpent,

> *"And I will put enmity between thee and the woman, and between thy seed and her seed; it shall bruise thy head, and thou shalt bruise his heel." Genesis 3:15*

When God made man He made him upright and good, but when sin entered it stripped man of his likeness to God and left him spiritually dead. God knew all of this and had already purposed what He would do to redeem His chosen ones from the penalty of sin. Paul explained it when he said,

> *"Blessed be the God and Father of our Lord Jesus Christ, who hath blessed us with all spiritual blessings in heavenly places in Christ: According as he hath chosen us in him before the foundation of the world, that we should be holy and without blame before him in love: Having predestinated us unto the adoption of children by Jesus Christ to himself, according to the good pleasure of his will, To the praise of the glory of his grace, wherein he hath made us accepted in the beloved." Ephesians 1:3-6*

God's purpose in all things is to receive glory for Himself. He said,

> *"For thus saith the high and lofty One that inhabiteth eternity, whose name is Holy; I dwell in the high and holy place, with him also that is of a contrite and humble spirit, to revive the spirit of the humble, and to revive the heart of the contrite ones." Isaiah 57:15*

He said,

> *"I am the LORD: that is my name: and my glory will I not give to another, neither my praise to graven images." Isaiah 42:8*

John said,

> *"Thou art worthy, O Lord, to receive glory and honour and power: for thou hast created all things, and for thy pleasure they are and were created." Revelation 4:11*

The way God receives maximum glory is through the work of the Son, Jesus Christ, the One He sent into the world to die for His lost sheep. When Jesus had completed the work assigned Him He said,

> *"Father, the hour is come; glorify thy Son, that thy Son also may glorify thee: As thou hast given him power over all flesh, that he should give eternal life to as many as thou hast given him. And this is life eternal, that they might know thee the only true God, and Jesus Christ, whom thou hast sent. I have glorified thee on the earth: I have finished the work which thou gavest me to do. And now, O Father, glorify thou me with thine own self with the glory which I had with thee before the world was." John 17:1-5*

THE FIRST OF THESE MOST IMPORTANT DAY WAS THE DAY OF HIS BIRTH

The Lord God told the serpent that the seed of the woman would bruise his head, but first the serpent would bruise His heel. When Jesus came into the world it was for the purpose of dying for His lost sheep. Paul said,

> *"But when the fulness of the time was come, God sent forth his Son, made of a woman, made under the law, To redeem them that were under the law, that we might receive the adoption of sons. And because ye are sons, God hath sent forth the Spirit of his Son into your hearts, crying, Abba, Father." Galatians 4:4-6*

The details of His birth were predicted by the Old Testament prophets. Isaiah tells us He was to be born of a virgin,

"Therefore the Lord himself shall give you a sign; Behold, a virgin shall conceive, and bear a son, and shall call his name Immanuel." Isaiah 7:14

Matthew tells us that Jesus was the fulfillment of that prophesy,

"But while he (Joseph) thought on these things, behold, the angel of the Lord appeared unto him in a dream, saying, Joseph, thou son of David, fear not to take unto thee Mary thy wife: for that which is conceived in her is of the Holy Ghost. And she shall bring forth a son, and thou shalt call his name JESUS: for he shall save his people from their sins. Now all this was done, that it might be fulfilled which was spoken of the Lord by the prophet, saying, Behold, a virgin shall be with child, and shall bring forth a son, and they shall call his name Emmanuel, which being interpreted is, God with us." Matthew 1:20-23

The place of His birth was foretold when the Lord said,

"But thou, Bethlehem Ephratah, though thou be little among the thousands of Judah, yet out of thee shall he come forth unto me that is to be ruler in Israel; whose goings forth have been from of old, from everlasting." Micah 5:2

When the wise men came to Jerusalem they said,

"Where is he that is born King of the Jews? for we have seen his star in the east, and are come to worship him. When Herod the king had heard these things, he was troubled, and all Jerusalem with him. And when he had gathered all the chief priests and scribes of the people together, he demanded of them where Christ should be born. And they said unto him, In Bethlehem of Judaea: for thus it is written by the prophet, And thou Bethlehem, in the land of Juda, art not the least among the princes

of Juda: for out of thee shall come a Governor, that shall rule my people Israel." Matthew 2:2-6

All of this marked the first of the three most important day of history, the day God became a man, it happened in BC 4. This fits perfectly with the time line God revealed to Daniel when, in a dream He said,

"Seventy weeks are determined upon thy people and upon thy holy city, to finish the transgression, and to make an end of sins, and to make reconciliation for iniquity, and to bring in everlasting righteousness, and to seal up the vision and prophecy, and to anoint the most Holy. Know therefore and understand, that from the going forth of the commandment to restore and to build Jerusalem unto the Messiah the Prince shall be seven weeks, and threescore and two weeks: the street shall be built again, and the wall, even in troublous times." Daniel 9:24-25

Counting from the time that Artaxerxes issued the decree to rebuild the temple in Jerusalem in BC 457 to the time Jesus was revealed to be the Son of God was 483 years, which matches the timeline revealed to Daniel perfectly. Jesus was about thirty years old when He was baptized and God said,

"This is my beloved Son, in whom I am well pleased."

The final seven years or the seventh week of Daniel covered the period of Jesus' earthly ministry or three and one half years, and three and one half years from His crucifixion and resurrection to the time Philip went into Gaza and preached to the eunuch. So, the 490 years of Daniel's dream were fulfilled. There is no valid reason to separate the final seven years from the first three hundred and eighty-three. This scheme was devised by those who invented the dispensational pre-millennial view, which was advanced by C. I. Scofield.

GOD BECAME A MAN

John said,

> *"And the Word was made flesh, and dwelt among us, (and we beheld his glory, the glory as of the only begotten of the Father,) full of grace and truth." John 1:14*

The writer to the Hebrews tells us,

> *"Forasmuch then as the children are partakers of flesh and blood, he also himself likewise took part of the same; that through death he might destroy him that had the power of death, that is, the devil; And deliver them who through fear of death were all their lifetime subject to bondage. For verily he took not on him the nature of angels; but he took on him the seed of Abraham. Wherefore in all things it behoved him to be made like unto his brethren, that he might be a merciful and faithful high priest in things pertaining to God, to make reconciliation for the sins of the people. For in that he himself hath suffered being tempted, he is able to succour them that are tempted." Hebrews 2:14-18*

Paul challenged the saints at Philippi to,

> *"Let this mind be in you, which was also in Christ Jesus: Who, being in the form of God, thought it not robbery to be equal with God: But made himself of no reputation, and took upon him the form of a servant, and was made in the likeness of men: And being found in fashion as a man, he humbled himself, and became obedient unto death, even the death of the cross." Philippians 2:5-8*

Jesus became one of us so that He might do for us what we could not do for ourselves. Paul said,

> *"For what the law could not do, in that it was weak through the flesh, God sending his own Son in the likeness of sinful flesh, and for sin, condemned sin in the flesh: That the righteousness of the law might be fulfilled in us, who walk not after the flesh, but after the Spirit." Romans 8:3-4*

Peter said of the perfect man Jesus,

> *"his own self bare our sins in his own body on the tree, that we, being dead to sins, should live unto righteousness: by whose stripes ye were healed." I Peter 2:24*

Had Jesus not come into the world as a man there could have been no salvation for Paul said,

> *"For there is one God, and one mediator between God and men, the man Christ Jesus; Who gave himself a ransom for all, to be testified in due time." I Timothy 2:5-6*

And Peter said,

> *"Neither is there salvation in any other: for there is none other name under heaven given among men, whereby we must be saved." Acts 4:12*

This is why I say that the day of His birth was one of the three most important days in human history.

THE DAY OF HIS DEATH AND RESURRECTION

The second of the most important days in history is the day of His death on the cross and His resurrection from Joseph's new tomb. Dying for His people was His primary purpose for coming into the world as a man. He said,

> *"For even the Son of man came not to be ministered unto, but to minister, and to give his life a ransom for many." Mark 10:45*

Jesus explained this to Nicodemus when He said,

> *"And as Moses lifted up the serpent in the wilderness, even so must the Son of man be lifted up:" John 3:14*

The cross was not an afterthought with God for Jesus was crucified according to,

> *"the determinate counsel and foreknowledge of God,"*

Peter said to the Jews,

> *"ye have taken, and by wicked hands have crucified and slain:" Acts 2:23*

Isaiah prophesied this when he said,

> *"Yet it pleased the LORD to bruise him; he hath put him to grief: when thou shalt make his soul an offering for sin, he shall see his seed, he shall prolong his days, and the pleasure of the LORD shall prosper in his hand." Isaiah 53:10*

John spoke of,

> *"the Lamb slain from the foundation of the world." Revelation 13:8*

When He was facing the shame and agony of the cross He said,

"Now is my soul troubled; and what shall I say? Father, save me from this hour: but for this cause came I unto this hour." John 12:27

Paul said Jesus,

"made himself of no reputation, and took upon him the form of a servant, and was made in the likeness of men: And being found in fashion as a man, he humbled himself, and became obedient unto death, even the death of the cross." Philippians 2:7-8

The writer to the Hebrews said,

"Looking unto Jesus the author and finisher of our faith; who for the joy that was set before him endured the cross, despising the shame, and is set down at the right hand of the throne of God." Hebrews 12:2

Paul said,

"Christ hath redeemed us from the curse of the law, being made a curse for us: for it is written, Cursed is every one that hangeth on a tree: That the blessing of Abraham might come on the Gentiles through Jesus Christ; that we might receive the promise of the Spirit through faith. Brethren, I speak after the manner of men; Though it be but a man's covenant, yet if it be confirmed, no man disannulleth, or addeth thereto." Galatians 3:13-15

And Paul added,

"For ye know the grace of our Lord Jesus Christ, that, though he was rich, yet for your sakes he became poor, that ye through his poverty might be rich." II Corinthians 8:9

HIS DEATH PLEASED THE FATHER

Isaiah said,

> *"Yet it pleased the LORD to bruise him; he hath put him to grief: when thou shalt make his soul an offering for sin, he shall see his seed, he shall prolong his days, and the pleasure of the LORD shall prosper in his hand. He shall see of the travail of his soul, and shall be satisfied: by his knowledge shall my righteous servant justify many; for he shall bear their iniquities. Therefore will I divide him a portion with the great, and he shall divide the spoil with the strong; because he hath poured out his soul unto death: and he was numbered with the transgressors; and he bare the sin of many, and made intercession for the transgressors." Isaiah 53:10-12*

The travail of His soul refers to the agony He endured while on the cross, dying for His lost sheep. His said,

> *"As many were astonied at thee; his visage was so marred more than any man, and his form more than the sons of men:" Isaiah 52:14*

He went on to say,

> *"For he shall grow up before him as a tender plant, and as a root out of a dry ground: he hath no form nor comeliness; and when we shall see him, there is no beauty that we should desire him. He is despised and rejected of men; a man of sorrows, and acquainted with grief: and we hid as it were our faces from him; he was despised, and we esteemed him not. Surely he hath borne our griefs, and carried our sorrows: yet we did esteem him stricken, smitten of God, and afflicted. But he was wounded for our transgressions, he was bruised for our iniquities: the chastisement of our peace was upon him; and with his stripes we are healed. All we like sheep have gone astray; we have turned every*

one to his own way; and the LORD hath laid on him the iniquity of us all. He was oppressed, and he was afflicted, yet he opened not his mouth: he is brought as a lamb to the slaughter, and as a sheep before her shearers is dumb, so he openeth not his mouth. He was taken from prison and from judgment: and who shall declare his generation? for he was cut off out of the land of the living: for the transgression of my people was he stricken." Isaiah 53:2-8

All the sins of His elect were laid on Him, but he was sufficient for the task. For where sin abounded, grace did much more abound. It is the grace of God that provided the sacrifice for our sins. Paul said,

"For by grace are ye saved through faith; and that not of yourselves: it is the gift of God: Not of works, lest any man should boast." Ephesians 2:8-9

He further said,

"Being justified freely by his grace through the redemption that is in Christ Jesus: Whom God hath set forth to be a propitiation through faith in his blood, to declare his righteousness for the remission of sins that are past, through the forbearance of God;" Romans 3:24-25

DEATH COULD NOT HOLD HIM

He died, but death could not hold Him for He said the Lord had made Him this promise,

"For thou wilt not leave my soul in hell; neither wilt thou suffer thine Holy One to see corruption." Psalm 16:10

Peter quoted this Psalm and said it concerned Jesus. He said,

> *"He seeing this before spake of the resurrection of Christ, that his soul was not left in hell, neither his flesh did see corruption. This Jesus hath God raised up, whereof we all are witnesses. Therefore being by the right hand of God exalted, and having received of the Father the promise of the Holy Ghost, he hath shed forth this, which ye now see and hear." Acts 2:31-33*

Paul made this victorious declaration,

> *"Knowing that Christ being raised from the dead dieth no more; death hath no more dominion over him. For in that he died, he died unto sin once: but in that he liveth, he liveth unto God." Romans 6:9-10*

He told Timothy,

> *"Be not thou therefore ashamed of the testimony of our Lord, nor of me his prisoner: but be thou partaker of the afflictions of the gospel according to the power of God; Who hath saved us, and called us with an holy calling, not according to our works, but according to his own purpose and grace, which was given us in Christ Jesus before the world began, But is now made manifest by the appearing of our Saviour Jesus Christ, who hath abolished death, and hath brought life and immortality to light through the gospel: Whereunto I am appointed a preacher, and an apostle, and a teacher of the Gentiles." II Timothy 1:8-11*

This is why Paul could say,

> *"O death, where is thy sting? O grave, where is thy victory? The sting of death is sin; and the strength of sin is the law. But thanks be to God, which giveth us the*

victory through our Lord Jesus Christ." I Corinthians 15:55-57

This was the second most important day in history for Jesus said,

"Yet a little while, and the world seeth me no more; but ye see me: because I live, ye shall live also." John 14:19

THE DAY OF HIS RETURN

Everyone agrees as to the time of the first two days, but when we speak of the third day, the day of His return, we meet resistance. It is sad to say that most preachers never mention this third day as an event that occurred in the day of our Lord, between BC 4 to AD 70, they still think of it as a future event yet to take place. Even though Jesus promised to return "shortly" and bring judgment upon Israel for her rejections of Him as the Messiah, many do not believe He came when He said He would. He said to His first century disciples,

*"Let not your heart be troubled: ye believe in God, believe also in me. In my Father's house are many mansions: if it were not so, I would have told you. I go to prepare a place for you. And if I go and prepare a place for you, **I will come again,** and receive you unto myself; that where I am, there ye may be also." John 14:1-3*

All the things He said would happen were to happen within that generation. He said very clearly several times,

*"Verily I say unto you, All these things shall come upon **this generation**." Matthew 23:36*

*"Verily I say unto you, **This generation** shall not pass, till all these things be fulfilled." Matthew 24:34*

When He returned He brought judgment on Israel and the kingdom was taken from her and given to a nation bringing forth the fruits thereof.

As God had always done with His people in the past, He gave Israel forty years to see her error and receive Jesus as the Messiah, but she did not. At the end of that probation period, when the transition from the Old covenant to the New covenant had been completed He did come in power and glory, using the Roman army as His angels of destruction and brought Old covenant Judaism to an end. The writer to the Hebrews mention this when he said,

"For if that first covenant had been faultless, then should no place have been sought for the second. For finding fault with them, he saith, Behold, the days come, saith the Lord, when I will make a new covenant with the house of Israel and with the house of Judah: Not according to the covenant that I made with their fathers in the day when I took them by the hand to lead them out of the land of Egypt; because they continued not in my covenant, and I regarded them not, saith the Lord. For this is the covenant that I will make with the house of Israel after those days, saith the Lord; I will put my laws into their mind, and write them in their hearts: and I will be to them a God, and they shall be to me a people: And they shall not teach every man his neighbour, and every man his brother, saying, Know the Lord: for all shall know me, from the least to the greatest. For I will

be merciful to their unrighteousness, and their sins and their iniquities will I remember no more. In that he saith, A new covenant, he hath made the first old. Now that which decayeth and waxeth old is ready to vanish away." Hebrews 8:7-13

We are no longer under the Old covenant and have to keep all its rigorous demands. We have been liberated, for Jesus kept it in our behalf and provided the righteousness required for entrance into heaven. Paul stated this to the church at Galatia. He said,

"Stand fast therefore in the liberty wherewith Christ hath made us free, and be not entangled again with the yoke of bondage. Behold, I Paul say unto you, that if ye be circumcised, Christ shall profit you nothing. For I testify again to every man that is circumcised, that he is a debtor to do the whole law. Christ is become of no effect unto you, whosoever of you are justified by the law; ye are fallen from grace. For we through the Spirit wait for the hope of righteousness by faith. For in Jesus Christ neither circumcision availeth any thing, nor uncircumcision; but faith which worketh by love." Galatians 5:1-6

When Paul wrote these words the Lord had not yet returned, but he knew that He had promised to return before that generation had passed. He wrote often of his expectation of the return of the Lord. He said to the Romans,

"And that, knowing the time, that now it is high time to awake out of sleep: for now is our salvation nearer than when we believed. The night is far spent, the day is at hand: let us therefore cast off the works of darkness, and let us put on the armour of light. Let us walk honestly, as in the day; not in rioting and drunkenness, not in chambering and wantonness, not in strife and

envying. But put ye on the Lord Jesus Christ, and make not provision for the flesh, to fulfil the lusts thereof." Romans 13:11-14

Every writing apostle believed and expected the Lord to return soon. That was the only generation that was correct when they said, "Jesus is coming soon." But there are still those who do not accept the fact that He did return in AD 70. All who have predicted His soon return since that time and have set dates saying they are able to read the signs of the times, have been proven wrong.

The blame for this can be laid at the feet of those who misunderstand the nature of His coming and alter the time statements to fit their expectations, rather than seeking to understand the nature of His coming from the time statements. The expectation of a literal bodily return has blinded the eyes of many, and they are still looking for something that has already occurred. Those who hold these views believe that when Jesus returns, He will destroy this world and will create a new one. They believe that this world is going to end. But the verses that speak of the end of the world (age) concern the end of the Jewish age, not of "terra firma."

The end of the Old Covenant age came when Jesus returned in power and glory and judged Israel and took the church as His bride. Instead of living for tomorrow and seeking to improve situations on the earth they long for the end of the earth as we know it and want something they already have in Jesus Christ. Whether you realize it or not, all those who are in Christ are living and reigning with Him on the earth right now.

An understanding of the importance of these three days will assist us in unlocking the message of Revelation. Failure to understand will leave one struggling to know what to expect in life. All that is described in Revelation has already taken place and it deals primarily with God's dealings with the nation of Israel. As John Noe' says,

"We are living beyond the end times."

Paul puts it so well when he says,

"For if by one man's offence death reigned by one; much more they which receive abundance of grace and of the gift of righteousness shall reign in life by one, Jesus Christ.)" Romans 5:17

What Adam lost; Jesus restored.

CHAPTER V

WHEN THE BOOK WAS OPENED

As John looked he saw,

"in the right hand of him that sat on the throne a book written within and on the backside, sealed with seven seals. And I saw a strong angel proclaiming with a loud voice, Who is worthy to open the book, and to loose the seals thereof? And no man in heaven, nor in earth, neither under the earth, was able to open the book, neither to look thereon. And I wept much, because no man was found worthy to open and to read the book, neither to look thereon. And one of the elders saith unto me, Weep not: behold, the Lion of the tribe of Juda, the Root of David, hath prevailed to open the book, and to loose the seven seals thereof." Revelation 5:1-5

The book that was sealed with seven seals was that which Daniel had been commanded to seal. After receiving the vision God said,

*"But thou, O Daniel, shut up the words, and seal the book, even to **the time of the end:** many shall run to and fro, and knowledge shall be increased." Daniel 12:4*

The time of the end had come for the writer to the Hebrews said,

*"God, who at sundry times and in divers manners spake in time past unto the fathers by the prophets, Hath in these **last days** spoken unto us by his Son, whom he hath appointed heir of all things, by whom also he made the worlds; Who being the brightness of his glory, and the express image of his person, and upholding all things by the word of his power, when he had by himself purged our sins, sat down on the right hand of the*

> *Majesty on high; Being made so much better than the angels, as he hath by inheritance obtained a more excellent name than they." Hebrews 1:1-4*

The *"last days"* spoken of by the writer to the Hebrews was the same time as that referred to as *"the time of the end"* to Daniel.   Jesus is then identified as the only one qualified to take the book and loose the seals and reveal what was written therein. He was,

> *"worthy to take the book, and to open the seals thereof: for thou wast slain, and hast redeemed us to God by thy blood out of every kindred, and tongue, and people, and nation;" Revelation 5:9*

THE TIME OF JUDGMENT HAS COME

When the book was opened John saw four horseman riding across the scene. They are figures of how judgment was coming on Israel for rejecting Jesus as Messiah.

The devastation described matches that spoken of by Jesus in the Olivet discourse. Jesus said that when judgment came men would say,

> *"to say to the mountains, Fall on us; and to the hills, Cover us." Luke 23:30*

The same words are uttered by the men mentioned by John as the horsemen rode through the land. John said,

> *"And I beheld when he had opened the sixth seal, and, lo, there was a great earthquake; and the sun became black as sackcloth of hair, and the moon became as blood; And the stars of heaven fell unto the earth, even*

as a fig tree casteth her untimely figs, when she is shaken of a mighty wind. And the heaven departed as a scroll when it is rolled together; and every mountain and island were moved out of their places. And the kings of the earth, and the great men, and the rich men, and the chief captains, and the mighty men, and every bondman, and every free man, hid themselves in the dens and in the rocks of the mountains; And said to the mountains and rocks, Fall on us, and hide us from the face of him that sitteth on the throne, and from the wrath of the Lamb: For the great day of his wrath is come; and who shall be able to stand?" Revelation 6:12-17

This is what happened in Israel when judgment fell in AD 70. From chapter six through chapter eleven John describes the judgment that fell as the seven seals were opened and the seven trumpets sounded. Josephus describes the horrors of this time in Jerusalem and all of the land of Israel in His account of the "Wars of the Jews."

One of the most convincing evidences for the book being written before AD 70 lies in the instructions given to John in chapter 11. John said,

"And there was given me a reed like unto a rod: and the angel stood, saying, Rise, and measure the temple of God, and the altar, and them that worship therein." Revelation 11:1

John could not have measured the temple after AD 70, for it had been destroyed.

Futurists say that another temple will be built in the "last days" and once again animal sacrifices will be offered. This would be the greatest insult to the once for all sacrifice Jesus made when He died on the cross. The futurists say they will just be memorial sacrifices, but a memorial to what, Jesus Himself will be there.

THE SEVENTH OR THE LAST TRUMPET SOUNDED

When the seventh trumpet sounded,

> *"there were great voices in heaven, saying, The kingdoms of this world are become the kingdoms of our Lord, and of his Christ; and he shall reign for ever and ever." Revelation 11:15*

This is what was promised to Jesus and was told to Daniel and to Mary. God said to Daniel,

> *"And in the days of these kings shall the God of heaven set up a kingdom, which shall never be destroyed: and the kingdom shall not be left to other people, but it shall break in pieces and consume all these kingdoms, and it shall stand for ever." Daniel 2:44*

To Mary, the angel Gabriel said,

> *"Fear not, Mary: for thou hast found favour with God. And, behold, thou shalt conceive in thy womb, and bring forth a son, and shalt call his name JESUS. He shall be great, and shall be called the Son of the Highest: and the Lord God shall give unto him the throne of his father David: And he shall reign over the house of Jacob for ever; and of his kingdom there shall be no end." Luke 1:30-33*

That reign is in effect today for Jesus,

> *"hath on his vesture and on his thigh a name written, **KING OF KINGS, AND LORD OF LORDS**." Revelation 19:16*

THE BEAST OUT OF THE SEA

When John wrote about the beast that arose out of the sea, he used code language. He describes, not some future man who will rise to prominence and be called the Anti-Christ and will rule the world during the so called future great tribulation, but rather he was talking about a cruel man who was alive at that time, his name was Nero, the wicked ruler of the Roman empire.

He used code language to prevent being killed for exposing the wickedness of Nero. Nero wreaked havoc in the world, especially Israel, until his untimely death. John identified him by using the symbolic number 666. As to the antichrist, John said at that time, during his lifetime,

> *"Little children, it is the last time: and as ye have heard that antichrist shall come, even now are there many antichrists; whereby we know that it is the last time." I John 2:18*

He did not confine antichrist to one person for he asked,

> *"Who is a liar but he that denieth that Jesus is the Christ? He is antichrist, that denieth the Father and the Son." I John 2:22*

And then he said,

> *"And every spirit that confesseth not that Jesus Christ is come in the flesh is not of God: and this is that spirit of antichrist, whereof ye have heard that it should come; and even now already is it in the world." I John 4:3*

"For many deceivers are entered into the world, who confess not that Jesus Christ is come in the flesh. This is a deceiver and an antichrist." II John 1:7

These are the only four verses in the whole Bible where antichrist is mentioned. He says clearly that anyone who denied that Jesus is the Christ is an antichrist. The idea that the world will see an actual man arise and deceive men and lead the world into destruction is not Biblical, it is the fruit of some man's imagination wresting the Scriptures to make them say what he wants them to say.

THE BATTLE OF ARMAGEDDON

The battle called the battle of Armageddon is also history. It was a time of war between the Romans and the Jews. There is not to be some future battle when the forces of good and evil will meet in actual physical combat. Paul tells us that our battle is not physical, but spiritual. He said to the church at Ephesus,

"For we wrestle not against flesh and blood, but against principalities, against powers, against the rulers of the darkness of this world, against spiritual wickedness in high places." Ephesians 6:12

THE FALL OF BABYLON

In chapters seventeen and eighteen John talks of the fall of Babylon. This is not the Babylon of old or Rome. It is Jerusalem. Jerusalem was spoken of as Babylon because of her wickedness in rejecting Jesus and calling for His crucifixion. The fall took place in AD 70 when the Roman army stormed the city and tore down the temple stone by stone, thus filling the prophecy of Jesus who said,

"See ye not all these things? verily I say unto you, There shall not be left here one stone upon another, that shall not be thrown down." Matthew 24:2

When the Romans attacked Jerusalem they set everything on fire including the temple. All the gold in the temple melted and ran into the cracks between the stones. The soldiers dismantled the stones to get the gold, thus fulfilling Jesus' prediction,

"there shall not be left here one stone upon another."

When Jerusalem fell Biblical Judaism came to an end. The kingdom was given to the church, the Lamb's wife.

THE MARRIAGE OF THE LAMB

Chapter nineteen details the marriage of the Lamb to His bride, the church. The church is composed of all those who have been washed in the blood of the Lamb and are *"arrayed in fine linen"* which is the righteousness of the saints. John said,

"And I heard as it were the voice of a great multitude, and as the voice of many waters, and as the voice of mighty thunderings, saying, Alleluia: for the Lord God omnipotent reigneth. Let us be glad and rejoice, and give honour to him: for the marriage of the Lamb is come, and his wife hath made herself ready. And to her was granted that she should be arrayed in fine linen, clean and white: for the fine linen is the righteousness of saints. And he saith unto me, Write, Blessed are they

which are called unto the marriage supper of the Lamb. And he saith unto me, These are the true sayings of God." Revelation 19:6-9

CHAPTER VI

THE THOUSAND YEARS AND THE NEW JERUSALEM

Without question the final three chapters of Revelation are the most challenging and the most misunderstood. It is with fear and trepidation that one seeks to handle them. Paul said,

> *"Therefore seeing we have this ministry, as we have received mercy, we faint not; But have renounced the hidden things of dishonesty, not walking in craftiness, nor handling the word of God deceitfully; but by manifestation of the truth commending ourselves to every man's conscience in the sight of God." II Corinthians 4:1-2*

Peter mentioned how difficult it is to understand certain portions of God's Word.   As he described the destruction of Jerusalem and the end of Biblical Judaism he said,

> *"Seeing then that all these things shall be dissolved, what manner of persons ought ye to be in all holy conversation and godliness, Looking for and hasting unto the coming of the day of God, wherein the heavens being on fire shall be dissolved, and the elements shall melt with fervent heat? Nevertheless we, according to his promise, look for new heavens and a new earth, wherein dwelleth righteousness. Wherefore, beloved, seeing that ye look for such things, be diligent that ye may be found of him in peace, without spot, and blameless. And account that the longsuffering of our Lord is salvation; even as our beloved brother Paul also according to the wisdom given unto him hath written*

*unto you; As also in all his epistles, speaking in them of these things; in which are **some things hard to be understood, which they that are unlearned and unstable wrest, as they do also the other scriptures, unto their own destruction.** Ye therefore, beloved, seeing ye **know** these things before, beware lest ye also, being led away with the error of the wicked, fall from your own stedfastness. But grow in grace, and in the knowledge of our Lord and Saviour Jesus Christ. To him be glory both now and for ever. Amen." II Peter 3:11-18*

WHAT ARE AND WHEN DID THE THOUSAND YEARS TAKE PLACE?

Is this to be taken as a literal number? Or is it a figure of speech? This is the only place in Scripture where a thousand-year reign is mentioned. But it is not said to be on the earth. I believe it is a symbolic number, much like the passage that says,

"For every beast of the forest is mine, and the cattle upon a thousand hills." Psalm 50:10

This is a reference to the time between Jesus' ascension back to the Father and His glorious return in judgment on Israel in AD 70.

During this time the Devil was restrained so that the gospel could go freely to all nations. Jesus' apostles were doing the work He commanded them to do and they preached the gospel to all known nations. It was most likely then when Jesus' statement about the apostles was fulfilled. He had said,

"Verily I say unto you, That ye which have followed me, in the regeneration when the Son of man shall sit in the throne of his glory, ye also shall sit upon twelve thrones, judging the twelve tribes of Israel." Matthew 19:28

The first resurrection was that event when Jesus descended into Sheol and led captivity free. The second resurrection was when all who died between His crucifixion and His return were raised. Since that time no one needs resurrection for Jesus said,

"I am the resurrection, and the life: he that believeth in me, though he were dead, yet shall he live: And whosoever liveth and believeth in me shall never die. Believest thou this?" John 11:25-26

If a believer shall never die, he has no need of resurrection.

The judgment was that event descried in Matthew twenty-five. Jesus said,

"When the Son of man shall come in his glory, and all the holy angels with him, then shall he sit upon the throne of his glory: And before him shall be gathered all nations: and he shall separate them one from another, as a shepherd divideth his sheep from the goats: And he shall set the sheep on his right hand, but the goats on the left. Then shall the King say unto them on his right hand, Come, ye blessed of my Father, inherit the kingdom prepared for you from the foundation of the world:" Matthew 25:31-34

"Then shall he say also unto them on the left hand, Depart from me, ye cursed, into everlasting fire, prepared for the devil and his angels:" Matthew 25:41

"And these shall go away into everlasting punishment: but the righteous into life eternal." Matthew 25:46

The saved were admitted to heaven, the lost were cast into hell. When Jesus died on the cross He paid the sin debt of all His elect and all who are in Him will never face judgment, for He said,

"Verily, verily, I say unto you, He that heareth my word, and believeth on him that sent me, hath everlasting life, and shall not come into condemnation [judgment]; but is passed from death unto life." John 5:24

Paul affirmed this when he said,

"There is therefore now no condemnation (judgment) to them which are in Christ Jesus, who walk not after the flesh, but after the Spirit. For the law of the Spirit of life in Christ Jesus hath made me free from the law of sin and death." Romans 8:1-2

WHAT HAPPENED TO THE DEVIL?

At the end of that time the devil was cast into the lake of fire. This was a part of Jesus' assignment. John said,

"Little children, let no man deceive you: he that doeth righteousness is righteous, even as he is righteous. He that committeth sin is of the devil; for the devil sinneth from the beginning. For this purpose the Son of God was manifested, that he might destroy the works of the devil." I John 3:7-8

The writer to the Hebrews said,

"Forasmuch then as the children are partakers of flesh and blood, he also himself likewise took part of the same; that through death he might destroy him that had

the power of death, that is, the devil; And deliver them who through fear of death were all their lifetime subject to bondage." Hebrews 2:14-15

Some say if the devil was destroyed why do we still see so much evil in the world today? It is not because of the devil, for Jesus said,

"For from within, out of the heart of men, proceed evil thoughts, adulteries, fornications, murders, Thefts, covetousness, wickedness, deceit, lasciviousness, an evil eye, blasphemy, pride, foolishness: All these evil things come from within, and defile the man." Mark 7:21-23

To try to blame all the evil in the world on the devil is not accurate. James said,

"Let no man say when he is tempted, I am tempted of God: for God cannot be tempted with evil, neither tempteth he any man: But every man is tempted, when he is drawn away of his own lust, and enticed. Then when lust hath conceived, it bringeth forth sin: and sin, when it is finished, bringeth forth death." James 1:13-15

Jeremiah said,

"The heart is deceitful above all things, and desperately wicked: who can know it?" Jeremiah 17:9

We all need a new heart, and only God can give it.

HERE COMES THE BRIDE

John then said,

"And I saw a new heaven and a new earth: for the first heaven and the first earth were passed away; and there

was no more sea. And I John saw the holy city, new Jerusalem, coming down from God out of heaven, prepared as a bride adorned for her husband. And I heard a great voice out of heaven saying, Behold, the tabernacle of God is with men, and he will dwell with them, and they shall be his people, and God himself shall be with them, and be their God. And God shall wipe away all tears from their eyes; and there shall be no more death, neither sorrow, nor crying, neither shall there be any more pain: for the former things are passed away. And he that sat upon the throne said, Behold, I make all things new. And he said unto me, Write: for these words are true and faithful." Revelation 21:1-5

"We must keep in mind that Revelation is a book of metaphors and symbols predicting events to take place in the first century and we must always interpret its passages with that fact in mind. Here is a verse that is nearly always misinterpreted because that fact is not kept in mind.

"And God shall wipe away all tears from their eyes; and there shall be no more death, neither sorrow, nor crying, neither shall there be any more pain: for the former things are passed away." Revelation 21:4

The symbolic language used here is the same as that used in the prophecy of Isaiah to describe the blessings of being freed from the captivity of Babylon. He said,

"And I will rejoice in Jerusalem, and joy in my people: and the voice of weeping shall be no more heard in her, nor the voice of crying." Isaiah 65:19

The cessation of weeping and crying could not mean a blessing enjoyed in heaven because the passage is about

Israel's national deliverance from Babylonian captivity. And it's the same in Revelation 21:4. *"No more death"* means no more persecution unto death. *"Neither sorrow nor crying"* had to do with the halting of the grief suffered by the saint over being persecuted. And *"no more pain"* pointed to the end of their troubles. What brought about these blessed conditions? There was no more death of martyrdom, no more grief of persecution, and no more tribulation because *"the former things [Jewish and pagan opposition] had passed away."* **"Revelation 17-22 Re-examined"** by George W. Bowman

When Jesus said,

> *"Behold, I make all things new"*

this was a way of saying that the Jewish nation, the old covenant and Judaism had been made obsolete. The new spiritual Israel was made up of all things new, this is what Paul meant when he said,

> *"Therefore if any man be in Christ, he is a new creature: old things are passed away; behold, all things are become new. And all things are of God, who hath reconciled us to himself by Jesus Christ, and hath given to us the ministry of reconciliation; To wit, that God was in Christ, reconciling the world unto himself, not imputing their trespasses unto them; and hath committed unto us the word of reconciliation. Now then we are ambassadors for Christ, as though God did beseech you by us: we pray you in Christ's stead, be ye reconciled to God. For he hath made him to be sin for us, who knew no sin; that we might be made the righteousness of God in him." II Corinthians 5:17-21*

Believers are free from the law of sin and death and live free in Christ Jesus. Paul said,

> *"There is therefore now no condemnation to them which are in Christ Jesus, who walk not after the flesh, but after the Spirit. For the law of the Spirit of life in Christ Jesus hath made me free from the law of sin and death." Romans 8:1-2*

Paul urged the saints in Galatia to,

> *"Stand fast therefore in the liberty wherewith Christ hath made us free, and be not entangled again with the yoke of bondage." Galatians 5:1*

What the law could not do for man Jesus did. Paul said,

> *"For what the law could not do, in that it was weak through the flesh, God sending his own Son in the likeness of sinful flesh, and for sin, condemned sin in the flesh: That the righteousness of the law might be fulfilled in us, who walk not after the flesh, but after the Spirit." Romans 8:3-4*

He went of to say,

> *"For Christ is the end of the law for righteousness to every one that believeth. For Moses describeth the righteousness which is of the law, That the man which doeth those things shall live by them. But the righteousness which is of faith speaketh on this wise, Say not in thine heart, Who shall ascend into heaven? (that is, to bring Christ down from above:) Or, Who shall descend into the deep? (that is, to bring up Christ again from the dead.) But what saith it? The word is nigh thee, even in thy mouth, and in thy heart: that is, the word of faith, which we preach; That if thou shalt confess with thy mouth the Lord Jesus, and shalt believe in thine heart that God hath raised him from the dead, thou shalt be saved. For with the heart man believeth unto*

righteousness; and with the mouth confession is made unto salvation. For the scripture saith, Whosoever believeth on him shall not be ashamed. For there is no difference between the Jew and the Greek: for the same Lord over all is rich unto all that call upon him." Romans 10:4-12

NEW WINE MUST BE PUT IN NEW BOTTLES

Jesus told His disciples,

"And no man putteth new wine into old bottles: else the new wine doth burst the bottles, and the wine is spilled, and the bottles will be marred: but new wine must be put into new bottles." Mark 2:22

The old wine was the law, the old bottle was Judaism under the old covenant. The new wine is the gospel of His saving grace. The new bottle is the church to whom the gospel has been entrusted to preach to every creature. The church is the new heaven and the new earth, the New Jerusalem, the holy city John saw coming down out of heaven.

The old heaven and earth passed away. Israel had been left desolate. Now the church stands front and center with the Lamb. All the enemies that had plagued her had been defeated and there would never be a time when she would be separated from His love. John put it like this,

"And I heard a great voice out of heaven saying, Behold, the tabernacle of God is with men, and he will dwell with them, and they shall be his people, and God himself shall be with them, and be their God." Revelation 21:3

Paul understood this and asked,

> *"Who shall separate us from the love of Christ? shall tribulation, or distress, or persecution, or famine, or nakedness, or peril, or sword? As it is written, For thy sake we are killed all the day long; we are ccounted as sheep for the slaughter. Nay, in all these things we are more than conquerors through him that loved us. For I am persuaded, that neither death, nor life, nor angels, nor principalities, nor powers, nor things present, nor things to come, Nor height, nor depth, nor any other creature, shall be able to separate us from the love of God, which is in Christ Jesus our Lord." Romans 8:35-39*

In these bodies of flesh we will continue to experience troubles and trials, but they are but temporary. The time is coming when we shall lay aside these bodies of sin and death and be clothed with a new body fashioned like the glorious body of our Lord. Paul cried out,

> *"O wretched man that I am! who shall deliver me from the body of this death? I thank God through Jesus Christ our Lord. So then with the mind I myself serve the law of God; but with the flesh the law of sin." Romans 7:24-25*

He then said,

> *"For our conversation is in heaven; from whence also we look for the Saviour, the Lord Jesus Christ: Who shall change our vile body, that it may be fashioned like unto his glorious body, according to the working whereby he is able even to subdue all things unto himself." Philippians 3:20-21*

John said,

"Behold, what manner of love the Father hath bestowed upon us, that we should be called the sons of God: therefore the world knoweth us not, because it knew him not. Beloved, now are we the sons of God, and it doth not yet appear what we shall be: but we know that, when he shall appear, we shall be like him; for we shall see him as he is. And every man that hath this hope in him purifieth himself, even as he is pure. Whosoever committeth sin transgresseth also the law: for sin is the transgression of the law." I John 3:1-4

REMAIN HERE FOR A WHILE

When Jesus lifted up His voice in His high priestly prayer He said,

"I have given them thy word; and the world hath hated them, because they are not of the world, even as I am not of the world. I pray not that thou shouldest take them out of the world, but that thou shouldest keep them from the evil. They are not of the world, even as I am not of the world. Sanctify them through thy truth: thy word is truth. As thou hast sent me into the world, even so have I also sent them into the world. And for their sakes I sanctify myself, that they also might be sanctified through the truth. Neither pray I for these alone, but for them also which shall believe on me through their word; That they all may be one; as thou, Father, art in me, and I in thee, that they also may be one in us: that the world may believe that thou hast sent me." John 17:14-21

Paul understood this and said,

"For to me to live is Christ, and to die is gain. But if I live in the flesh, this is the fruit of my labour: yet what I shall choose I wot not. For I am in a strait betwixt two, having

a desire to depart, and to be with Christ; which is far better: Nevertheless to abide in the flesh is more needful for you. And having this confidence, I know that I shall abide and continue with you all for your furtherance and joy of faith; That your rejoicing may be more abundant in Jesus Christ for me by my coming to you again." Philippians 1:21-26

HIS AMBASSADORS

The Lord leaves us in the world for a season after He saves us that we might serve Him and tell others about Him. Paul said,

"Now then we are ambassadors for Christ, as though God did beseech you by us: we pray you in Christ's stead, be ye reconciled to God. For he hath made him to be sin for us, who knew no sin; that we might be made the righteousness of God in him." II Corinthians 5:20-21

There will always be a body of believers on the earth and they will have teachers to tell them the things of God and His Christ. Paul said to Timothy,

"And the things that thou hast heard of me among many witnesses, the same commit thou to faithful men, who shall be able to teach others also. II Timothy 2:2

I learned from those who taught me, you can now learn from those whom God has given you as your spiritual teachers.

The church will always be on the earth for Paul said,

"Unto him be glory in the church by Christ Jesus throughout all ages, world without end. Amen." Ephesians 3:21

The church exists in two realms. The visible church, that is those of us who are still in these bodies of flesh on the earth and the invisible church are those who have put off the body of flesh and have been clothed with their new body. Paul said,

"For we know that if our earthly house of this tabernacle were dissolved, we have a building of God, an house not made with hands, eternal in the heavens. For in this we groan, earnestly desiring to be clothed upon with our house which is from heaven: If so be that being clothed we shall not be found naked." II Corinthians 5:1-3

THE VISIBLE AND THE INVISIBLE

Paul describes both aspects in the letter to the Colossians. He says,

*"Giving thanks unto the Father, which hath made us meet to be partakers of the inheritance of the saints in light: Who hath delivered us from the power of darkness, and hath translated us into the kingdom of his dear Son: In whom we have redemption through his blood, even the forgiveness of sins: Who is the image of the invisible God, the firstborn of every creature: For by him were all things created, that are in heaven, and that are in earth, **visible and invisible,** whether they be thrones, or dominions, or principalities, or powers: all things were created by him, and for him: And he is before all things, and by him all things consist. And he is the head of the body, the church: who is the beginning, the firstborn from the dead; that in all things he might have*

the preeminence. For it pleased the Father that in him should all fulness dwell; And, having made peace through the blood of his cross, by him to reconcile all things unto himself; by him, I say, whether they be things in earth, or things in heaven." Colossians 1:12-20

As Jesus closed the Revelation he said,

"I Jesus have sent mine angel to testify unto you these things in the churches. I am the root and the offspring of David, and the bright and morning star. And the Spirit and the bride say, Come. And let him that heareth say, Come. And let him that is athirst come. And whosoever will, let him take the water of life freely." Revelation 22:16-17

SEAL NOT THE SAYINGS OF THIS BOOK

When God showed Daniel what was to come at the time of the end He said,

"Go thy way, Daniel: for the words are closed up and sealed till the time of the end." Daniel 12:9

The seals were not opened until one of the elders said to John,

"Weep not: behold, the Lion of the tribe of Juda, the Root of David, hath prevailed to open the book, and to loose the seven seals thereof." Revelation 5:5

As the seals were opened the events shown to Daniel regarding the things that were coming upon the nation of Israel transpired. Daniel said,

"And whiles I was speaking, and praying, and confessing my sin and the sin of my people Israel, and

*presenting my supplication before the LORD my God for the holy mountain of my God; Yea, whiles I was speaking in prayer, even the man Gabriel, whom I had seen in the vision at the beginning, being caused to fly swiftly, touched me about the time of the evening oblation. And he informed me, and talked with me, and said, O Daniel, I am now come forth to give thee skill and understanding. At the beginning of thy supplications the commandment came forth, and **I am come to shew thee; for thou art greatly beloved: therefore understand the matter, and consider the vision. Seventy weeks are determined upon thy people and upon thy holy city,** to finish the transgression, and to make an end of sins, and to make reconciliation for iniquity, and to bring in everlasting righteousness, and to seal up the vision and prophecy, and to anoint the most Holy. Know therefore and understand, that from the going forth of the commandment to restore and to build Jerusalem unto the Messiah the Prince shall be seven weeks, and threescore and two weeks: the street shall be built again, and the wall, even in troublous times. And after threescore and two weeks shall Messiah be cut off, but not for himself: and the people of the prince that shall come shall destroy the city and the sanctuary; and the end thereof shall be with a flood, and unto the end of the war desolations are determined. And he shall confirm the covenant with many for one week: and in the midst of the week he shall cause the sacrifice and the oblation to cease, and for the overspreading of abominations he shall make it desolate, even until the consummation, and that determined shall be poured upon"* Daniel 9:20-27

Jesus showed to John what was about to happen to Israel. Divine judgment was coming because of their sins and the rejection of His Son, Jesus Christ. All that is written in Revelation is what God had decreed. When Jesus had given John the Revelation. He then said,

> *"Seal not the sayings of the prophecy of this book: for the time is at hand." Revelation 22:10*

Unlike that which was shown to Daniel six hundred years earlier, when there was to be a delay in the fulfillment of the things shown, John was to leave the book unsealed for **the time was at hand**. Everything recorded in Revelation was future when John received it, but it is now history to us. Jesus said,

> *"For these be the days of vengeance, that **all things which are written may be fulfilled.**" Luke 21:22*

All came to pass and was finished when the Roman army destroyed the temple and the city bringing the Old covenant of Judaism to an end.

HIS FINAL WORD

The last thing Jesus said was,

> *"He which testifieth these things saith, Surely I come quickly. Amen."*

John said,

> *"Even so, come, Lord Jesus." Revelation 22:20*

And he did not disappoint. Just as He promised He came in power and glory in the clouds and judged wicked Israel and took the church to be His wife. That is the message of Revelation.

WHY NOT USE THE KEY?

The key that unlocks the Revelation is to know and believe that what Jesus showed John was to be done **shortly.** If we deny this and force the events to sometime in the future, then we lose the significance the message had for those to whom it was given. We must keep in mind that the Bible was written for us, but not to us. Audience relevance is vital in rightly dividing the Word of God.

THIS IS A BEAUTIFUL BOOK

While some say that Revelation is a horrible book because of the things described therein, I believe it is a beautiful book for it shows the faithfulness of God to always keep His word. He told the people of Israel that if they would keep His covenant and serve Him that He would bless them, but if they broke His covenant and followed after other "gods" He would curse them. Read Deuteronomy 28. God is true to His word. What He has said He will do. He closes the book with this warning,

> *"For I testify unto every man that heareth the words of the prophecy of this book, If any man shall add unto these things, God shall add unto him the plagues that are written in this book: And if any man shall take away from the words of the book of this prophecy, God shall take away his part out of the book of life, and out of the holy city, and from the things which are written in this book." Revelation 22:18-19*

But if we go back to the first chapter of the book God says,

> *"Blessed is he that readeth, and they that hear the words of this prophecy, and keep those things which are written therein: for the time is at hand." Revelation 1:3*

Are you blessed or cursed when you read the Revelation?

I John 4:19

Books by Dr. Jimmy Henry

- **There Is A Better Way**
  A study of Hebrews showing the transition from the Old Covenant to the New Covenant
- **Eyewitnesses Of His Majesty**
  A Biblical view of the return of Jesus Christ
- **Is The Rapture Past Or Future?**
  An Examination of the Removal of the Church
- **GOD's Indestructible World**
  A Biblical View Of Two Ages
- **GOD's Indescribable Heaven**
  A Biblical View Of Heaven
- **The Bride The Lamb's Wife**
  A Biblical View Of The Bride Of Christ
- **Promises Made Promises Kept**
  A Study of God's Promises to His People
- **One GOD and One LORD**
  A study of the attributes of the Only True God
- **The Key That Unlocks Revelation**
  An examination of the word "shortly"

For description and purchase information please visit:

www.GoodBookCrib.com